Headstart Ma

addition, subtraction, multiplication & division

Shirley Clarke & Barry Silsby
Illustrated by Sascha Lipscomb

Test 1   Growing families
Test 2   Adding
Test 3   Fly away home
Test 4   Balloon pop
Test 5   Subtracting
Test 6   Word sums
Test 7   Picture sums
Test 8   Make a number
Test 9   Up to 10 number race
Test 10   Crack the code
Test 11   What's the difference?
Test 12   Which coins?
Test 13   Number patterns
Test 14   Tables square
Test 15   More word sums
Test 16   Tables tombola
Test 17   Halves and quarters
Test 18   Dividing
Test 19   Up to 20 number race

Answers and ways to help

Notes for parents

Each activity in this book tests your child.
 It will show you what your child is achieving, and advise on how you can help improve your child's performance. Do remember that your child's teacher will be able to tell you a great deal more about his or her ability.

How you can help
You can support your child in the following ways:

* make sure he/she knows what the instructions mean, reading them out or explaining them in your own words.

* encourage your child to 'try things out' if he/she feels unsure of the answer, either on scrap paper or by talking it through.

* don't put your child under pressure. The activities in this book are designed to be fun, and your child will benefit from doing, discussing and enjoying them.

* if your child gets stuck, try saying 'What do you think the answer may be?'

* always emphasise how well your child has done, particularly pointing out when he/she has got close to the right answer.

* talk to your child about the symbols at the end of each test, which help him or her to begin self-assessment. This is what they mean:

How much did you like doing this?			How much help did you need?		
a lot	a bit	not much	a lot	a bit	not much

Ask your child to circle one of the three faces, and one of the three hands. Children perform best when they are enjoying what they are doing, and can do many things with help which they cannot do alone. Selecting the appropriate symbol will help you and your child to assess both these factors.

TEST 1
Growing families

Count how many there are in each family and write the answer in the box.

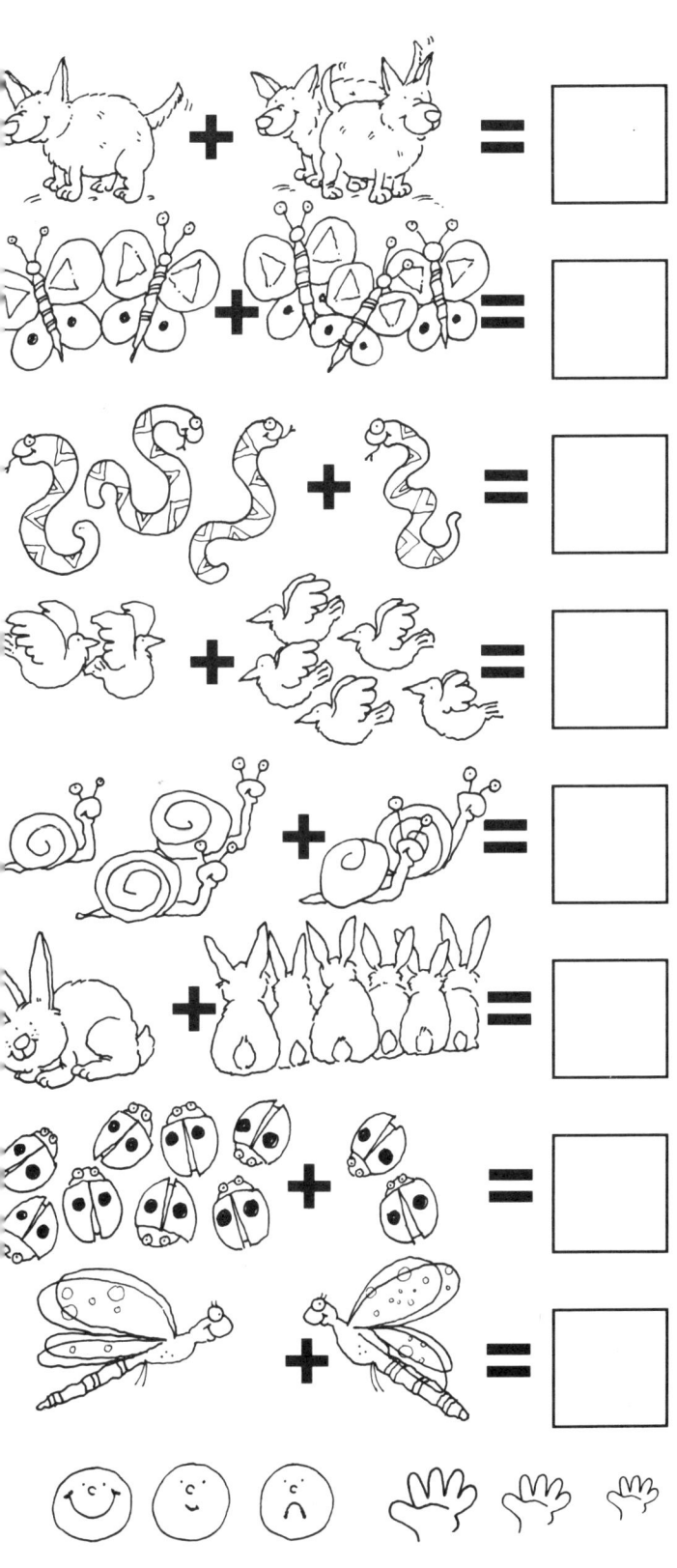

TEST 2

Adding

Work out the answers to these sums. Use your fingers or anything else as counters.

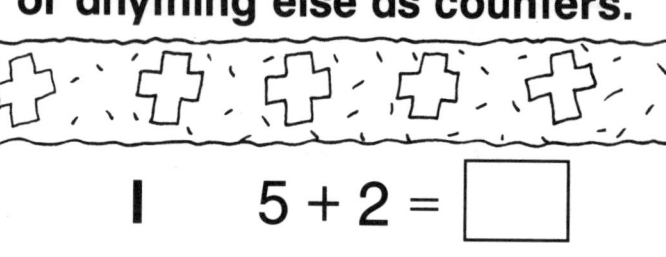

1.   5 + 2 = ☐
2.   1 + 3 = ☐
3.   2 + 2 = ☐
4.   5 + 5 = ☐
5.   2 + 3 = ☐
6.   4 + 0 = ☐
7.   6 + 2 = ☐
8.   7 + 3 = ☐
9.   8 + 1 = ☐
10.   4 + 3 = ☐

TEST 3
Fly away home

5 ladybirds on a leaf.   **1** flies away home.

Draw how many are left.

3 ladybirds on a leaf.   **2** fly away home.

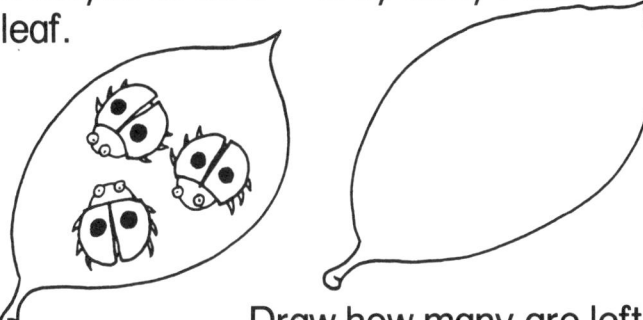

Draw how many are left.

7 ladybirds on a leaf.   **3** fly away home.

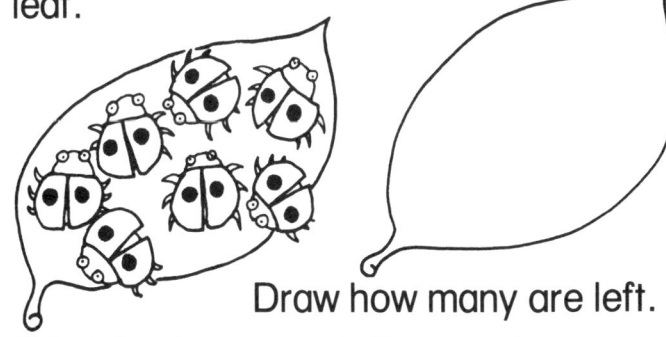

Draw how many are left.

2 ladybirds on a leaf.   **2** fly away home.

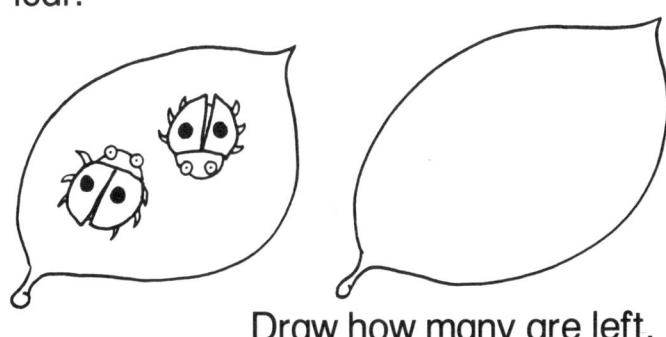

Draw how many are left.

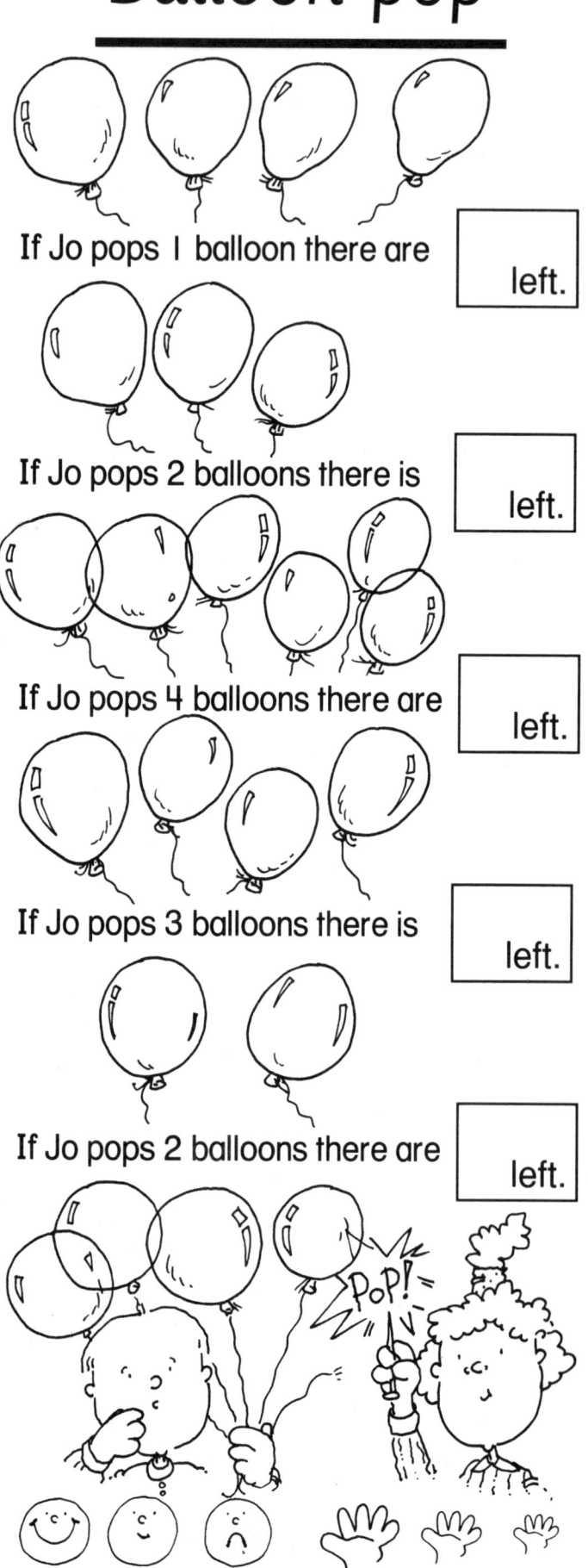

TEST 4
Balloon pop

If Jo pops 1 balloon there are ☐ left.

If Jo pops 2 balloons there is ☐ left.

If Jo pops 4 balloons there are ☐ left.

If Jo pops 3 balloons there is ☐ left.

If Jo pops 2 balloons there are ☐ left.

TEST 5
Subtracting

Work out the answers to these sums. You can use your fingers, counters or anything to help you count.

1. 3 − 2 = ☐
2. 5 − 4 = ☐
3. 4 − 2 = ☐
4. 2 − 1 = ☐
5. 6 − 3 = ☐
6. 8 − 5 = ☐
7. 9 − 1 = ☐
8. 10 − 5 = ☐
9. 4 − 4 = ☐
10. 5 − 2 = ☐

TEST 6
Word sums

Tick the right answer.

1. 10 people on a bus. 7 more get on. How many people are on the bus altogether?

   | 3 | 17 | 20 |

2. I spend 13p, then 10p, then 5p. How much have I spent altogether?

   | 30p | 15p | 28p |

3. I have 21 sweets. I give away 19. How many do I have left?

   | 40 |
   | 3 |
   | 2 |

4. In my pocket I have a 50p coin, a 2p coin and a 20p coin.

   How much money have I got?

   | 52p | 62p | 72p |

5. 300 people wanted to see a film. 100 couldn't get in. How many saw the film?

   | 100 |
   | 200 |
   | 400 |

TEST 7
Picture sums

2 dogs live here.   5 dogs live here.

3 dogs live here.

How many dogs altogether? ☐

25 biscuits in this pack.

Tina eats 10 biscuits. How many left? ☐

15 new apples grow on this tree.

How many then? ☐

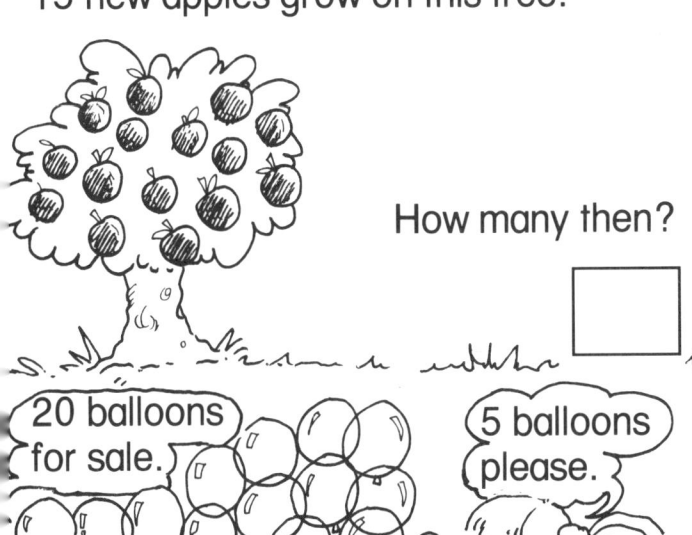

20 balloons for sale.

5 balloons please.

How many balloons left? ☐

TEST 8

Make a number

Put numbers in the boxes to complete these sums. The first one has already been done.

1. [2] + [3] + [1] = 6

2. ☐ + ☐ = 5

3. ☐ - ☐ = 2

4. ☐ + ☐ + ☐ = 8

5. ☐ - ☐ = 5

6. ☐ + ☐ = 9

7. ☐ + ☐ + ☐ + ☐ = 10

8. ☐ - ☐ = 3

1 4 0 7 8

TEST 9

Up to 10 number race

How fast can you do these sums? Get someone to time you and check the answers.

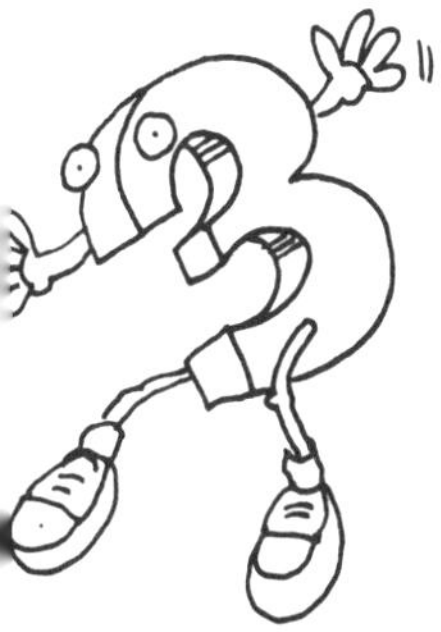

1. 2 + 3 = ☐
2. 4 + 4 = ☐
3. 5 + 1 = ☐
4. 4 + 5 = ☐
5. 6 + 4 = ☐
6. 3 + 4 = ☐
7. 4 - 1 = ☐
8. 7 - 4 = ☐
9. 10 - 5 = ☐
10. 9 - 3 = ☐
11. 6 - 2 = ☐
12. 8 - 4 = ☐

Rub out the answers or cover them up and try again. See if you can get quicker each time.

First try	Second try	Third try
time	time	time

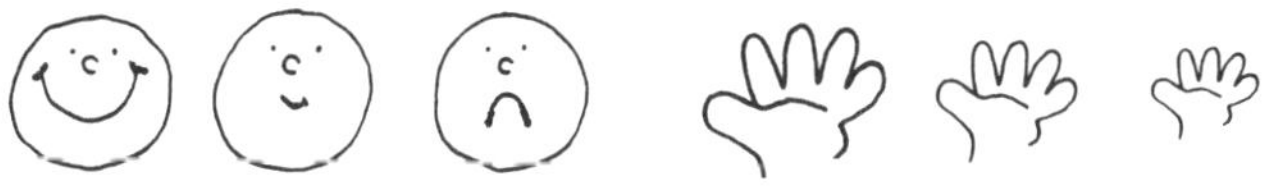

TEST 10

Crack the code

In each of these lines the ★ stands for a secret number. Can you crack the code?

1
| 1 | 2 | 3 | ★ | 5 | 6 | ★ =

2
10 - ★ = 4   ★ =

3
100 + 100 = ★   ★ =

4
| ★ | 4 | 6 | 8 | 10 | 1★ | ★ =

5
| 10 | 20 | ★ | 40 | 50 | ★ =

6
6 + ★ = 14   ★ =

7
| 5 | 10 | 15 | ★ | 25 | ★ =

8
★ + ★ = 10   ★ =

TEST 11

What's the difference?

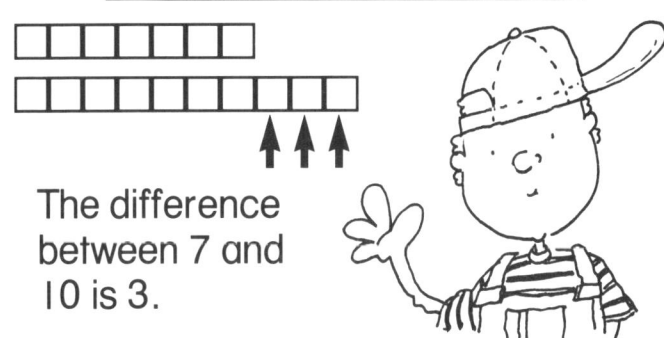

The difference between 7 and 10 is 3.

What is the difference between these numbers?

1 The difference between 6 and 4 is ____.

2 The difference between 2 and 10 is ____.

3 The difference between 3 and 5 is ____.

4 The difference between 10 and 20 is ____.

5 The difference between 15 and 17 is ____.

6 The difference between 12 and 20 is ____.

7 The difference between 19 and 30 is ____.

8 The difference between 100 and 50 is ____.

TEST 12
Number patterns

Here are all the ways to make 5 by adding numbers together.

5	+	0	or	0	+	5
4	+	1	or	1	+	4
3	+	2	or	2	+	3

Do the following in the same way.

All the ways to make **6** by adding.

☐ + ☐ or ☐ + ☐

☐ + ☐ or ☐ + ☐

☐ + ☐ or ☐ + ☐

3 + 3

All the ways to make **7** by adding.

☐ + ☐ or ☐ + ☐

☐ + ☐ or ☐ + ☐

☐ + ☐ or ☐ + ☐

☐ + ☐ or ☐ + ☐

All the ways to make **8** by adding.

☐ + ☐   or   ☐ + ☐

☐ + ☐   or   ☐ + ☐

☐ + ☐   or   ☐ + ☐

☐ + ☐   or   ☐ + ☐

☐ + ☐

All the ways to make **9** by adding.

☐ + ☐   or   ☐ + ☐

☐ + ☐   or   ☐ + ☐

☐ + ☐   or   ☐ + ☐

☐ + ☐   or   ☐ + ☐

☐ + ☐   or   ☐ + ☐

All the ways to make **10** by adding.

☐ + ☐   or   ☐ + ☐

☐ + ☐   or   ☐ + ☐

☐ + ☐   or   ☐ + ☐

☐ + ☐   or   ☐ + ☐

☐ + ☐   or   ☐ + ☐

☐ + ☐

TEST 13

Which coins?

Tick the exact coins you would need to pay for each toy. The first one has been done for you.

TEST 14

Table square

Fill in the missing numbers. Check with an adult if you are not sure how a table square works.

X	1	2	3	4	5
1	1	2		4	5
2	2	4		8	
3	3		9		15
4	4			16	
5	5		15		25

TEST 15

More word sums

Tick the right answer.

1. 8 children have 5p each.
   How much do they have altogether?

   | 40p | 4p | 14p |

2. 21 biscuits are shared by 7 people.
   How many do they each get?

   | 7 | 3 | 14 |

3. The hall has 10 rows with 10 seats in each row.
   How many people can sit down?

   | 1000 | 20 | 100 |

4. I have 8 sausages to share between 4 people.
   How many do they each get?

   | 32 | 2 | 4 |

5. I have 3 50p pieces.
   How much do I have altogether?

   | £3.50 | £1.50 | £150 |

TEST 16
Tables tombola

All of these tickets have won prizes. Join the ticket to the prize.

TEST 17

Halves and quarters

Tick the correct answer.

1 Half of 50p

| 25p | 20p | 5p |

2 Quarter of 12 cm

| 4 cm | 3 cm | 6 cm |

3 Half of 80

| 40 | 20 | 60 |

4 Quarter of £1

| 50p | 25p | 75p |

5 Half of 16

| 2 | 4 | 8 |

6 Half of 200

| 50 | 100 | 400 |

7 Quarter of 8

| 2 | 4 | 6 |

8 Quarter of 20

| 4 | 5 | 10 |

9 Half of 1 hour

| 15 minutes |
| 20 minutes | 30 minutes |

10 Quarter of 16

| 4 | 8 | 12 |

TEST 18

Dividing

Decide whether these numbers can be divided exactly by 2, 5 and/or 10. Tick which they can be divided by. The first one has been done for you.

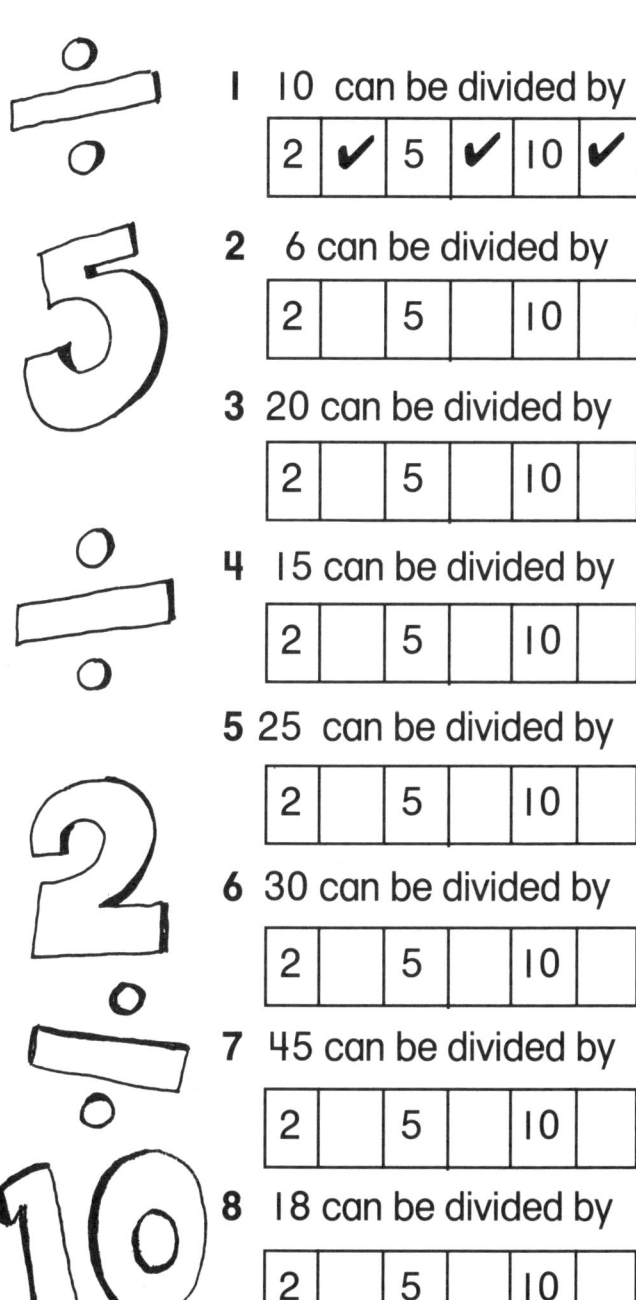

1 10 can be divided by

| 2 ✔ | 5 ✔ | 10 ✔ |

2 6 can be divided by

| 2 | 5 | 10 |

3 20 can be divided by

| 2 | 5 | 10 |

4 15 can be divided by

| 2 | 5 | 10 |

5 25 can be divided by

| 2 | 5 | 10 |

6 30 can be divided by

| 2 | 5 | 10 |

7 45 can be divided by

| 2 | 5 | 10 |

8 18 can be divided by

| 2 | 5 | 10 |

TEST 19

Up to 20 number race

How fast can you do these sums? Get someone to time you and check the answers.

1. 8 + 5 =
2. 11 + 3 =
3. 9 + 4 =
4. 10 + 5 =
5. 16 + 3 =
6. 7 + 8 =
7. 15 - 2 =
8. 11 - 9 =
9. 17 - 6 =
10. 19 - 4 =
11. 20 - 9 =
12. 13 - 7 =

Rub out the answers or cover them up and try again. See if you can get quicker each time.

First try	Second try	Third try
time	time	time

Answers
and ways to help

Test 1 Growing families
3, 5, 4, 7, 5, 7, 10, 2
Help by encouraging your child to count by pointing to each creature one by one.

Test 2 Adding
1 7 2 4 3 4 4 10 5 5 6 4 7 8
8 10 9 9 10 7
Help by using counters and moving them one at a time as they are counted.

Test 3 Fly away home
4, 1, 4, 0
Help by crossing off the ones which fly away and helping your child to count the rest.

Test 4 Balloon pop
3, 1, 2, 1, 0,
Help by crossing off the popped balloons.

Test 5 Subtracting
1 1 2 1 3 2 4 1 5 3 6 3 7 8 8 5 9 0
10 3
Help by using counters and moving them as they are subtracted.

Test 6 Word sums
1 17 2 28p 3 2 4 72p 5 200
Help by encouraging your child to estimate what the answer might be, then looking at the answers. Use real money, counters or bricks to work out the answers.

Test 7 Picture sums
10, 15, 30, 15
Help by using counters, fingers or marks on paper.

Test 8 Make a number
Uses any numbers which makes the total.
Help by using counters and splitting them into groups. Check that the numbers used make the total.

Test 9 Up to 10 number race
1 5 2 8 3 6 4 9 5 10 6 7 7 3 8 3 9 5
10 6 11 4 12 4
Help by playing games with two dice, where you add up or take away the two numbers thrown as quickly as possible.

Test 10 Crack the code
1 4 2 6 3 200 4 2 5 30 6 8 7 20 8 5
Help by reading out the numbers, so that the sequence is more obvious.

Test 11 What's the difference?
1 2 **2** 8 **3** 2 **4** 10 **5** 2 **6** 8 **7** 11 **8** 50
<ins>Help</ins> by using counters or bricks lined up as in the picture.

Test 12 Number Patterns
6=6+0 or 0+6   **7**=7+0 or 0+7   **8**=8+0 or 0+8
   5+1 or 1+5   6+1 or 1+6   7+1 or 1+7
   4+2 or 2+4   5+2 or 2+5   6+2 or 2+6
   3+3   4+3 or 3+4   5+3 or 3+5
                                                         4+4

9=9+0 or 0+9   **10**= 10+0 or 0+10
   8+1 or 1+8   9+1 or 1+9   <ins>Help</ins> by getting
   7+2 or 2+7   8+2 or 2+8   your child
   6+3 or 3+6   7+3 or 3+7   started, as in the
   5+4 or 4+5   6+4 or 4+6   example, and by
                          5+5   pointing out the
                                           pattern.

Test 13 Which coins?
Uses any combination of coins which added together make the prices.
<ins>Help</ins> by using real coins and showing how to start by counting large numbers first.

Test 14 Table square
3, 6, 10, 6, 12, 8, 12, 20, 10, 20
<ins>Help</ins> by pointing out the patterns made down and across by each number.

Test 15 More word sums
1 40p **2** 3 **3** 100 **4** 2 **5** £1.50
<ins>Help</ins> by getting your child to estimate first. Divide out counters or bricks to make the answers.

Test 16 Tables tombola
1x5 = 5 3x3 = 9 2x6 = 12 5x5 = 25 4x2 = 8
4x4 = 16 5x3 = 15 9x2 = 18
<ins>Help</ins> by referring to or making a tables square.

Test 17 Halves and quarters
1 25p **2** 3 cm **3** 40 **4** 25p **5** 8 **6** 100 **7** 2
8 5 **9** 30 mins **10** 4
<ins>Help</ins> by getting your child to estimate first. Use counters or bricks to split the numbers into halves or quarters.

Test 18 Dividing
2 2 **3** 2,5,10 **4** 5 **5** 5 **6** 2,5,10 **7** 5 **8** 2
<ins>Help</ins> by explaining that the number might be able to be divided by 2 or 5 or 10, or combinations of any two or all three numbers. Use counters to see if the numbers will divide into 2, 5 or 10 and refer to a tables square.

Test 19 Up to 20 number race
1 13 **2** 14 **3** 13 **4** 15 **5** 19 **6** 15 **7** 13
8 2 **9** 11 **10** 15 **11** 11 **12** 6
<ins>Help</ins> by encouraging your child to have several goes, in order to memorise number facts.